MW01205961

Table of Contents

Introduction

Garlic is the second most widely used cultivated Allium after onion. It has long been recognized all over the world as a valuable spice for foods and a popular remedy for various ailments and physiological disorders. It is grown throughout Pakistan and consumed by most of the people.

History Of Garlic

Few foods have been enjoyed for such a long period of time and in so many different parts of the world as garlic. There is evidence that garlic originally grew wild in locations as diverse as China, India, Egypt, and what is now Ukraine. At the present time, because wild garlic only grows prolifically in the area represented by Kyrgyzstan, Tajikistan, Turkmenistan, and Uzbekistan, this region is considered by some to be the "center of origin" for this remarkable food. Regardless of its center of origin, however, garlic has been cultivated for thousands of years in diverse regions of the world and has become a staple in cuisines across many continents.

China is by far the world's largest commercial producer of garlic, with 20 million tons of production in 2014. In that same year, India was the second largest producer with about 1.25 million tons, and South Korea, Egypt, and Russia rounded out the top five countries for garlic production. Between 50-75% of all garlic consumed in the U.S. is currently grown in China. Mexico and Argentina are also important sources for garlic imports into the U.S. At present, the U.S. serves as the number one import market for fresh garlic worldwide. This demand for fresh garlic in the U.S. is clearly reflected in our increased history of use: on a per capita basis, U.S. adults average about 2 pounds of garlic per year, as compared with less than ½ pound per year in the early 1970's.

Within the United States, 80-90% of all garlic comes from California. Two regions of the state are especially important for garlic production: the western San Joaquin Valley and the area west of the Diablo mountain range. Much smaller amounts of garlic are grown commercially in Oregon, Nevada, and Arizona.

Garlic

Garlic has a high concentration of sulfur-containing compounds. Thiosulfinates, which include allicin, are the main active components in garlic. It also contains:

- High levels of saponins, phosphorus, potassium, sulfur, and zinc
- Moderate levels of selenium and vitamins A and C

- Low levels of calcium, magnesium, sodium, iron, manganese, and B-complex vitamins

Purported Health Benefits Of Garlic

Though there is a solid amount of small-scale, low-quality research about garlic, proper clinical trials are lacking. Thus, most of the purported health benefits of garlic have not been proven.

Possibly Effective for:

Hardening of the Arteries (Atherosclerosis)

Heart disease is associated with high cholesterol, high blood pressure, increased platelet aggregation, and the hardening of blood vessels. Platelets stop bleeding by clotting blood vessel injuries. However, platelet aggregation also leads to blood clots, which increase the risk of heart disease.

Limited evidence suggests that garlic may lower cholesterol, reduce blood pressure, relax hardened blood vessels, and prevent platelet aggregation in patients with heart disease. This is uncertain and large-scale studies are needed.

S-allyl cysteine in aged garlic extract inhibits enzymes involved in cholesterol production. Garlic extract also increases the production and function of nitric oxide, which relaxes blood vessels and lowers blood pressure. Garlic also prevents platelets from binding to proteins (fibrinogen) that form blood clots and increase compounds (cAMP) that inhibit platelet formation.

Blood Sugar Control in Diabetes

Diabetes is caused by genetics, obesity, high cholesterol, blood pressure, or blood glucose. Insulin resistance occurs when the body no longer responds to insulin, leading to increased blood sugar levels and a high risk of developing diabetes.

According to some researchers, garlic might reduce insulin resistance, blood sugar, and cholesterol levels in patients with diabetes. Some clinical studies suggest that garlic might slightly lower pre-meal blood sugar levels, particularly if taken for at least 3 months in people diabetes. More research is needed.

Garlic reduced blood sugar levels in rats by decreasing the activity of enzymes (phosphatases and aminotransferases) involved in the transportation of glucose in the liver, a sugar that is the body's main source of energy.

Also, garlic may reduce insulin resistance by inhibiting an enzyme that breaks down drugs (CYP2E1), ultimately disrupting insulin function by increasing oxidative stress.

High Blood Fats (Hyperlipidemia)

According to limited studies, garlic lowers total and low-density lipoprotein (LDL) cholesterol by inhibiting cholesterol synthesis in the liver in human and animal studies. Garlic lowered cholesterol by deactivating cholesterol-producing enzymes in 70 diabetic patients.

However, the evidence about garlic's cholesterol-lowering effect is mixed. According to the NIH, even if garlic does lower blood cholesterol, "the effect is small, and low-density lipoprotein (LDL) cholesterol (the so-called 'bad' cholesterol that's linked to increased heart disease risk) may not be reduced at all."

High Blood Pressure

Garlic reduces blood pressure in patients with high blood pressure (hypertension). Aged garlic extract reduces blood pressure by increasing calcium and reducing C-reactive protein levels, which cause inflammation and elevated blood pressure.

On the other hand, sulfur deficiency may play a role in hypertension. Allicin is a sulfur compound in garlic that lowers blood pressure by increasing hydrogen sulfide concentrations. Hydrogen sulfide relaxes blood vessels (through nitric oxide) and prevents blood vessel constriction (by endothelin-1).

Certain Yeast Infections

Small clinical trials suggest that applying a gel with garlic (containing 0.6% ajoene) twice daily may improve the following yeast infections within a week:

- Ringworm (Tinea corporis)
- Jock itch (Tinea cruris)
- Athlete's foot (Tinea pedis)

Repelling Ticks

Garlic seems to be a promising insect repellent, but just how well it works compared to standard synthetic repellents is still unknown. In one study, people who ate a lot of garlic (1200 mg daily) over 8 weeks seemed to have fewer tick bites, compared to placebo.

Prostate Cancer Prevention

Findings on the effects of dietary garlic intake on prostate cancer prevention have been mixed.

A link between higher garlic intake (over 2 grams/day) and lower prostate cancer risk has been suggested in Chinese men. Also, early clinical studies suggest that garlic supplements may help prevent prostate cancer.

S-allyl cysteine and SAMC inhibit prostate cancer cell growth by re-activating E-cadherin, a molecule that suppresses tumor invasion, in cancer patients. A low level of E-cadherin is associated with a high number of tumors and poor prognosis in prostate cancer patients.

Although classified as possibly effective for prostate cancer prevention based on the existing evidence, larger clinical trials are needed.

Likely Ineffective For:

Ulcers Caused By H. pylori

Raw garlic has antibacterial effects against H. pylori, the most common bacterial infection in the world and the main cause of ulcers in human and animal studies. Allicin in garlic reacts with proteins resulting in the inhibition of pathways associated with inflammation (TLR4 and NF-kB).

Garlic oil soothes ulcers in rats by increasing the concentration of antioxidant enzymes and by inhibiting proteins that cause inflammation. However, studies failed to demonstrate the benefits of garlic extract against H. pylori in humans. Therefore, the exisiting evidence suggests that garlic likely doesn't help with ulcers caused by this common bacteria.

Cancer

According to the National Center for Complementary and Integrative Health (NIH): "Some studies indicate that certain groups of people who eat more garlic may be less likely to develop certain cancers, such as stomach and colon cancers. However, garlic in dietary supplement form has not been shown to help reduce the risk of these cancers. The National Cancer Institute recognizes garlic as one of several vegetables with potential anticancer properties but does not recommend using garlic dietary supplements for cancer prevention."

S-allylmercaptocysteine (SAMC), a sulfur compound in garlic, was hypothesized to affect cancer cells in cell-based studies. Scientists say that SAMC appears to bind to a protein involved in cell reproduction (tubulin), activating proteins (JNK1 and caspase-3) that, theoretically, cause tumor cell death. However, most clinical studies have failed to show effectiveness.

Breast Cancer

Diallyl disulfide in garlic seemed to prevent the growth of breast tumors. It was hypothesized to promote tumor cell death and inhibit tumor growth (via Bcl-2 proteins and the enzyme caspase) in rats.

In human studies, however, taking garlic by mouth did not reduce the risk of developing breast cancer.

Lung Cancer

Diallyl trisulfide was thought to work in combination with the chemotherapy drug cisplatin to inhibit lung tumor growth in mice. Diallyl trisulfide activated pathways that cause tumor cell death and prevents tumor cell growth (p53, Bcl-2, JNK, p38, and caspase). But in humans, taking garlic did not contribute to lung cancer prevention.

Stomach Cancer

Researchers hypothesized that S-allylmercaptocysteine (SAMC) in garlic may suppress the growth of stomach tumors in rats. They claimed that SAMC cauased tumor cell death by activating the enzymes caspase and protein kinases (MAPK and PI3K/Akt).

However, the most reliable evidence from human studies did not find an association between garlic intake and stomach cancer prevention.

Garlic has an antimicrobial effect on bacteria, yeast, fungi, parasites, and viruses. Allicin and sulfur-containing compounds in garlic inhibit DNA, RNA, and protein production in microbes.

Effect On The Cold And Flu

In a study (DB-RCT) of 120 individuals, aged garlic extract reduced the severity of colds and the flu by increasing the number of immune cells (T cells and NK cells) and by boosting the immune system. Aged garlic extract increases the activity of immune cells while lowering inflammatory proteins (cytokines).

However, solid evidence is still lacking to determine whether garlic can help fight the cold and fly. Larger, better-designed studies are needed.

Lacking Evidence for:

No clinical evidence supports the use of garlic for any of the conditions listed in this section.

Below is a summary of the existing animal and cell-based research, which should guide further investigational efforts.However, the studies listed below should not be interpreted as supportive of any health benefit.

Boosting the Immune System

In animal and cell-based studies, aged garlic extract stimulates white blood cells (lymphocytes, macrophages, monocytes, and neutrophils) by increasing glutathione. White blood cells are immune cells that provide protection against infections, while glutathione is an antioxidant that protects immune cells from free radicals.

Candida Yeast Infections

In petri-dish studies, fresh garlic extract inhibited the growth of Candida, the most common type of yeast infections. Allicin in garlic inhibits the growth of candida by destroying fats present

in the outer surface of the yeast. We can't draw any conclusions from cell-based studies; both animal and human studies are lacking to back up this purported health benefit.

Preventing Tooth Decay and Oral Infections

Garlic has antibacterial effects on dental plaque bacteria that cause tooth decay if left untreated. Scientists think garlic may also help with oral infections like periodontitis, oral thrush, and sore mouth from dentures. Some researchers believe it should be researched in conjunction with antibiotics.

Allicin in garlic is hypothesized to harm bacteria by inhibiting sulfur-containing enzymes that bacteria need for survival.

Possible Effects On HIV

In a cell-based study, diallyl disulfide in garlic inhibited cell growth and selectively killed HIV-infected immune cells. Diallyl disulfide also inhibits virus replication by decreasing the production of proteins involved in HIV replication.

Ajoene, a garlic extract, prevents normal blood cells from fusing with HIV-infected cells and inhibits HIV replication in infected cells.ajoene may prevent cell fusion by inactivating platelet integrins (a protein that causes blood cells to fuse together) in the blood.

However, these findings only relate to cell-based studies. Animal studies are lacking.what's more, we can't determine the potential effects of garlic on HIV until proper clinical trials are carried out.

Intestinal Infections Caused By Parasites

Some scientists believe garlic has the potential to help with parasitic intestinal infections like giardiasis and tapeworm infections, based on studies in rats.

Allicin in garlic disrupts the mobility, food absorption, and reproduction of the parasites by blocking fat synthesis in the parasites.garlic also promotes immune function and strengthens the body's defense mechanism against parasitic infections by stimulating white blood cells.

Brain Cancer

Diallyl trisulfide, a sulfur-containing compound in garlic, decreases the size of brain tumors in mice by inhibiting the enzyme histone deacetylase (HDAC), which causes tumor cell death.

Esophageal Cancer

Diallyl sulfide in garlic inhibits esophagus tumor formation in rats by disrupting the energy production of NMBA, which is a chemical found in fungi-contaminated foods that can cause liver and esophagus cancer.

Progression Of Skin Cancer

Allyl sulfides in garlic control the growth of human skin cancer cells by causing DNA damage in cancer cells in human studies. The DNA damage in cancer cells signals the p53 protein to stop cancer cell growth and to kill cancer cells.

Liver Cancer Progression

Sulfur compounds in garlic inhibit liver cancer cell growth by activating proteins (p53, p21, and JNK) that stop tumor cell growth and cause cell death in rats

Colon Cancer Progression

Diallyl disulfide and S-allylmercaptocysteine (SAMC) in garlic suppress colon tumor growth by stopping cancer cell growth and increasing tumor cell death in cell and rat studies.

Diallyl disulfide disrupts the tumor cell cycle by activating the protein ERK.SAMC, which increases tumor cell death by activating the protein JNK1 and the enzyme caspase.

Bladder Cancer

Garlic inhibits bladder tumor growth by stimulating immune cells and detoxifying carcinogens in mice.garlic increases the activity of macrophages and lymphocytes, which attack tumor cells.garlic detoxifies carcinogens by activating the antioxidant enzyme CYP2E1.

Allergies

Aged garlic extract suppressed allergic reactions in mice.ethyl acetate in aged garlic extract may directly suppress the immune protein FceRI, which is associated with the release of inflammatory factors during allergy responses. Aged garlic extract prevents inflammation during allergic reactions by inhibiting the release of histamine.

Skin Protection from Ultraviolet Rays

Garlic protects the skin from ultraviolet (UV) radiation by stimulating immune cells in human studies.

When exposed to UV rays, the urocanic acid in the skin changes, which causes suppression of the immune system. Aged garlic extract lessens the suppression of immune cells by decreasing the concentration of urocanic acid in rats.

Anti-Aging Effects

Long-term topical treatment with garlic extract may have anti-aging effects since garlic increases the growth and lifespan of skin cells. Garlic-treated skin cells are more healthy compared to untreated cells. Antioxidants in garlic prevents damage caused by free radicals. Garlic also contains cytokinin, a hormone that promotes cell growth and delays aging through its antioxidant effects.

Skin Rash

Garlic may soothe skin rashes like psoriasis and eczema.Activation of the compound NF-kB has been linked to skin rashes. NF-kB, which is activated by free radicals, cancer-causing agents, and UV light, causes inflammation.S-allyl cysteine in garlic suppresses the pathway of NF-kB by inhibiting free radicals and lowering oxidative stress in cell model and human studies.

Scars

Garlic helps with keloid scars, which are tough scars caused by the overgrowth of skin collagen. Garlic inhibits growth factors, nitric oxide, and enzymes involved in the production of collagen.

Hair Loss

Some scientists think garlic gel in combination with steroid cream might be good for patients suffering from alopecia, a type of hair loss that results from immune cells attacking hair follicles. Diallyl disulfide in garlic may prevent the autoimmune response and induce hair re-growth by increasing immune suppressor cells.

Obesity

Garlic prevents obesity by reducing body weight and fat accumulation in mice studies. In animal studies, garlic activates proteins (AMPK and uncoupling proteins) in fat tissue, liver, and muscle, which converts nutrients into heat instead of energy storage.

Ajoene, a compound found in garlic, prevents obesity by decreasing fat tissue in rats. Ajoene generates hydrogen peroxide, which activates enzymes (protein kinases) that kill fat cells.

Detoxification By the Liver

Toxins like pesticides, environmental pollutants, and chemicals cause oxidative stress and inflammation in the body. Garlic detoxifies the body through its antioxidant effects. Sulfur-containing compounds in garlic decrease oxidative stress and reduce inflammation in rats.

Garlic detoxifies the liver by increasing the activity of detoxifying enzymes glutathione S-transferase (GST) and CYP2B. Garlic also inhibits CYP2E1 enzymes, which produce free radicals and cause oxidative stress-induced damage and inflammation.

Damage Caused By Liver Toxicity

Garlic powder protects against damage from liver toxicity caused by high doses of antibiotics, Tylenol, and lead in rat studies. Garlic acts as an antioxidant and prevents oxidative stress by stabilizing free radicals. The decrease in oxidative stress may increase the activity of antioxidant enzymes, which prevents further damage to the liver.

Damage Caused By Kidney Toxicity

Garlic helped with kidney failure caused by the antibiotic gentamicin and kidney damage caused by cisplatin, a chemotherapy drug, in rats.

S-allyl cysteine, a sulfur compound in garlic, acts as an antioxidant by inhibiting free radicals, which cause cellular damage in the body. By lowering free radicals, it increases the activity of antioxidant enzymes in the kidney. S-allyl cysteine also inhibits the enzymes that produce free radicals.

Potential Effects On The Aging Brain & Brain Diseases

Free radicals are highly unstable molecules that are formed when oxygen is used in the body to produce energy. Bodily antioxidants inhibit free radicals by stabilizing the molecules.

Without enough antioxidants, free radicals cause cellular damage in the body.

S-allyl cysteine is an antioxidant found in aged garlic extract that protects against brain damage in a cell model study. S-allyl cysteine activates antioxidant enzymes in the brain (hippocampus) that decreases free radicals preventing damage.

Memory

Garlic increases brain serotonin, a neurotransmitter that enhances cognitive performance. Garlic oil improves memory function and cognitive performance in rats by increasing neuronal growth.

Side Effects And Precautions

Although garlic consumption is safe, ingested garlic can cause bad breath and body odor. Consuming an excessive amount of raw garlic, especially on an empty stomach, may lead to an upset stomach, gas, and changes in intestinal bacteria.

Handling garlic during cooking and topical application of garlic can cause allergic skin rashes, burns, and blisters.

Due to its anti-blood-clotting abilities, a high dose of garlic has an interaction with blood thinners like aspirin and warfarin.

Garlic supplements should be stopped seven days before surgical procedures to prevent any complications.

TRPV1 Gene

Mutations in the transient receptor potential V1 (TRPV1) gene may cause hypersensitivity to allicin in garlic extract in humans. The TRPV1 gene is found throughout the nervous system, bladder, tongue, and skin.

The mutations in the gene might cause structural changes in the TRPA1 protein, making it more sensitive to allicin. The TRPA1 protein is an allicin receptor that triggers inflammation and a pain response when activated.

Black Garlic

Aged black garlic is a garlic preparation with a sweet and sour taste and no strong odor.

Aged black garlic is produced by aging garlic at high temperature for two to three weeks. It contains high levels of organic sulfur compounds like water-soluble S-allyl cysteine and polyphenols.

Aged black garlic has stronger antioxidant effects than raw fresh garlic, but lower anti-inflammatory, anticoagulation, anti-allergy, and immune effects.

Dosage And Supplements

Garlic supplements are classified into four groups:

- Garlic oil: Water-soluble compounds and allicin are eliminated by this process. It contains a variety of sulfides, including diallyl disulfide
- Garlic oil macerate: Made of encapsulated garlic cloves ground into vegetable oil. Oil macerate contains allicin, which decomposes quickly into other compounds (dithiins, ajoene, and sulfides)
- Garlic powder: Dried and pulverized into powder. The main sulfur compound in garlic powder is alliin. Garlic powder does not contain allicin
- Aged garlic extract: Aged raw garlic has an increased concentration of antioxidant compounds. Allicin decomposes into other compounds, including S-allyl cysteine, which is one of the most active compounds in aged garlic extract

- For adults, the recommended amount is 4 grams (1 to 2 cloves) of raw garlic, 300 mg dried garlic powder tablet 2 to 3 times or 7.2 grams of garlic extract per day.

- Alliin, an amino acid containing sulfur, is broken down by the enzyme alliinase and converted to allicin when raw garlic is chopped or crushed. Allicin is an unstable compound that degrades quickly, so be sure to chop your garlic right before uses.

- Cooked garlic is less potent than raw garlic because the enzymes that form sulfur compounds are deactivated by heat

Garlic's Effects On Heart Health

According to the CDC, heart disease continues to be the leading cause of death for both men and women in the US, and it is a major cause of death throughout the world. Since February is American

Heart Month, it's time to start thinking about how you can reduce your risk of heart disease—your diet is a great place to start! Garlic contains a sulfur compound known as allicin that is formed when garlic cloves are crushed, chewed, or chopped.

Allicin is responsible for most of the health benefits you reap from garlic.

Clinical studies have shown that garlic/allicin can have a wide range of health benefits, many of which are specific to your heart health. One way garlic can help your heart health is by improving your cholesterol levels—lowering both the total level and the LDL (or "bad cholesterol") number. If you already have high cholesterol, supplementing with garlic could reduce your LDL and total cholesterol by as much as 10 to 15 percent.

Incorporating more garlic into your diet can be easy! Try adding chopped cloves to sautéed greens such as broccoli, kale, and spinach. Potatoes can be roasted with whole garlic cloves and then sprinkled with your favorite seasoning, and crushed or chopped garlic goes great with almost all Italian dishes.

From reducing blood pressure to lowering levels of bad cholesterol, the health advantages of adding more garlic to your diet can aid in the prevention of heart disease and heart-related conditions, such as a heart attack.

A Hint of Caution

But many studies showing a cardiovascular benefit, though rigorous, are small, and not every study shows that garlic is beneficial. There has even been concern that garlic supplements may be harmful for some people with heart disease.

A research review published in the Journal of the American College of Cardiology found that garlic (along with green tea, ginkgo, ginseng, and hawthorn) can interfere with the efficacy of some heart medications or increase their side effects.

For example, too much garlic can pose a bleeding risk for people on anticoagulants such as warfarin (Coumadin, Panwarfin) or a prescribed aspirin regimen. It may also make some other drugs less effective, such as saquinavir, a drug used to treat HIV infection, according to the National Institutes of Health.

The research is even weaker for garlic's ability to fight bacteria, ward off colds, boost the immune system, or reduce the risk of certain cancers, such as stomach or colon cancer.

"There's a lot of purported benefits of these medicines [garlic supplements]," says Budoff at the Los Angeles Biomedical Research Institute. "I'm more comfortable with the research on the cardiovascular benefits of garlic, and I'm less comfortable with it curing the common cold, acting as an antiviral, or other therapies."

Garlic In Your Dinner

Perhaps for these reasons, experts say the best way to get your garlic is from the fresh clove, although there can be a few "side effects" from eating it fresh. Garlic breath is probably the worst of it, but some people do suffer from indigestion after eating fresh garlic.

A less stinky and easier-on-the-stomach alternative may be black garlic, which is "aged" under intense heat and humidity for 10 days, turning the bulbs black and purportedly giving the allium a sweeter, more sour taste with a jelly-like consistency. This aging process rids the garlic of its pungent, irritating properties, but the benefits remain.

Garlic is an essential part of the Mediterranean diet, "which has been shown to have the best long-term outcomes of any diet we know of," says Budoff. Studies have linked this way of eating—which emphasizes produce, legumes, grains, and healthy oils, with small amounts of fish and meat—to a better quality of life, a lower risk of chronic disease, and better brain health in older adults.

"I use garlic in a lot of recipes," says Ellen Klosz, a Consumer Reports nutritionist. "You can use it to spice up a healthy dish without having to add any salt. Just make sure to use fresh garlic instead of garlic salt, which will boost the sodium levels."

How To Get The Most Out Of Garlic

- **Choose the freshest bulbs**

Look for plump bulbs with tight skin that isn't frayed, loose, dried out, or moldy. Sprouting, too, is a sign of age. The fresher the garlic, the higher the concentration of its active ingredients. Though garlic can keep for months; he says it's best to eat it within a week. "If you go longer than that, you can end up with something that's deactivated.

- **Store it right**

Keep garlic in a cool, dark place with good ventilation to prevent it from getting moldy or from sprouting.

Chop it for your health

Chopping, slicing, or smashing garlic triggers an enzyme reaction that increases its healthful compounds. Heat prevents this reaction, so let garlic sit on the cutting board for at least 10 minutes before cooking.

Minimize garlic breath

The smell of garlic can stay on your breath and be excreted by the lungs for a day or two after you eat it. A study published in the Journal of Food Science in 2016 suggests that munching on raw mint leaves, apples, or lettuce after a garlicky meal can help by neutralizing the sulfur compounds in garlic responsible for its odor.

Other Potential Health Benefits of Garlic

As mentioned in the section above, sulfur-containing compounds in garlic have been shown to support our body's detox processes, especially processes involving sulfur or the role of glutathione-S-transferase (GST) enzymes. Also of special interest in this detox area has been the potential role of garlic's allyl sulfides.

The antibacterial, antiviral, and antifungal properties of garlic are fairly well studied, although not necessarily within the context of human diseases and their development. And like the cancer studies on garlic, most of these antimicrobial studies have involved the use of garlic supplements rather than its food form. Due to the strong research interest in garlic and gastric cancer, several studies have examined the potential for garlic compounds to help prevent overgrowth of the bacterium Helicobacter pylori in the stomach or overadherence of this bacterium to the stomach wall. However, results in this area have been mixed. In several studies, the ajoenes present in garlic have been successfully used to help prevent infections with the yeast Candida albicans. We have also see a study showing the ability of crushed fresh garlic to help prevent infection by the bacterium Pseudomonas aeruginosa in burn patients.

One exciting new area of research involves the potential role of garlic to support bone health. As mentioned earlier in this article, the diallyl disulfides (DADS) in garlic have been identified as the garlic compounds that help protect our cardiovascular system from damage by cigarette smoke. With respect to bone health, studies have shown that cigarette smoking increases our risk of osteoporosis, inadequate bone mineral density, and inability to heal from bone fractures. Conversely, intake of garlic may be able to reduce risk of these problems by offsetting some of the potential damage caused by chronic exposure to cigarette smoke. Especially interesting in this context is the potential of garlic to help protect osteoblast cells from damage. Osteoblasts are bone cells that help produce new bone matrix. If garlic intake can help protect these cells from potential damage by cigarette smoke, it may be able to help support formation of new bone matrix and maintenance of existing bone structure.

A final promising area of research on the potential health benefits of garlic involves blood sugar regulation. One focus in this area involves a hormone released by our fat cells called adiponectin. When there is too little adiponectin in our blood, our risk of type 2 diabetes and certain cardiovascular problems gets increased. In what we would describe as preliminary studies, 12 weeks of garlic consumption has been shown to increase blood levels of adiponectin in human participants. Researchers believe that this process may be closely connected with simultaneous production of another key regulatory molecule called nitric oxide. While more follow-up studies are needed, these initial results show a potential for garlic intake to lower our risk of type 2 diabetes through what would be called hormone-related pathways. We have also seen a recent research showing significant decreases in fasting blood sugar levels following garlic intake. The authors of this research actually combined results together from seven previous studies to do a more robust analysis of the garlic-fasting blood sugar relationship. In their conclusions, these researchers suggested further confirmation of blood sugar impacts by examining other markers of blood sugar regulation including PPG (postprandial glucose, i.e., the amount of sugar in our blood following a meal) and hemoglobin A1C (the percent of red blood cells to which sugar becomes attached).

How to Select and Store

For maximum flavor and nutritional benefits, always purchase fresh garlic. Although garlic in flake, powder, or paste form may be more convenient, you will derive less culinary and health benefits from these forms.

Purchase garlic that is plump and has unbroken skin. Gently squeeze the garlic bulb between your fingers to check that it feels firm and is not damp.

Avoid garlic that is soft, shriveled, and moldy or that has begun to sprout. These may be indications of decay that will cause inferior flavor and texture. Size is often not an indication of quality. If your recipe calls for a large amount of garlic, remember that it is always easier to peel and chop a few larger cloves than many smaller ones.

Store fresh garlic in either an uncovered or a loosely covered container in a cool, dark place away from exposure to heat and sunlight. This will help maintain its maximum freshness and help prevent sprouting, which reduces its flavor and causes excess waste. It is not necessary to refrigerate garlic. Some people freeze peeled garlic; however, this process reduces its flavor profile and changes its texture.

Depending upon its age and variety, whole garlic bulbs will keep fresh for about a month if stored properly. Inspect the bulb frequently and remove any cloves that appear to be dried out or moldy. Once you break the head of garlic, it greatly reduces its shelf life to just a few days.

Tips For Preparing And Cooking

The first step to using garlic is to separate the individual cloves. An easy way to do this is to place the bulb on a cutting board or hard surface and gently, but firmly, apply pressure with the palm of your hand at an angle. This will cause the layers of skin that hold the bulb together to separate.

Peel garlic with a knife or alternatively, separate the skin from the individual cloves by placing a clove with the smooth side down on a cutting board and gently tapping it with the flat side of a wide knife. You can then remove the skin either with your fingers or with a small knife. If there is a green sprout in the clove's center, gently remove it since it is difficult to digest.

You can find lively discussions about garlic's sulfur compounds, its enzymes, and the best way to prepare this allium vegetable. Some of garlic's health benefits have been linked to a particular sulfur-containing compound called allicin. Allicin is produced when an enzyme in garlic called alliinase breaks down another sulfur-containing compound in garlic called alliin. The crushing of raw garlic greatly increases the chance for this alliin-to-allicin conversion to take place. For this reason, some people prefer to crush raw garlic cloves in a garlic press when using garlic in a cooked dish. When garlic is being enjoyed in raw form, this same crushing garlic can take place not with a garlic press, but with thorough chewing.

The Nutrient-Rich Way of Cooking Garlic

If it is a cooked dish that you are preparing and you cannot tolerate raw garlic, add chopped garlic towards the end of the cooking time to retain better flavor.

How to Enjoy

Recipes That Feature Garlic:

- Garlic Shrimp Salad
- Mediterranean Dressing

We actually include garlic as an ingredient in so many of our recipes. To find these just go to the Recipe Assistant on the Recipes page and click on "garlic" in the "Food to Include" box.

A Few Quick Serving Ideas;

- Purée fresh garlic, canned garbanzo beans, tahini, olive oil and lemon juice to make quick and easy hummus dip.
- Healthy Sauté steamed spinach, garlic, and fresh lemon juice.
- Add garlic to sauces and soups.
- Purée roasted garlic, cooked potatoes and olive oil together to make delicious garlic mashed potatoes. Season to taste.

Nutritional Profile

The sulfur compounds in garlic serve as its spotlight nutrients. These compounds include thiosulfinates, sulfoxides, sulfides, diallyl sulfides and polysulfides, vinyldithiins, ajoenes, and sulfur-containing amino acids and peptides. In addition, garlic is an excellent source of manganese and vitamin B6; a very good source of vitamin C and copper; and a good source of selenium, phosphorus, vitamin B1 and calcium.

Garlic Home Remedies

Sore Throat

Garlic is an invaluable medicine for asthma, hoarseness, coughs, difficulty of breathing, and most other disorders of the lungs, being of particular virtue in chronic bronchitis, on account of its powers of promoting expectoration.

Asthma

An older remedy for asthma, that was most popular, is a syrup of Garlic, made by boiling the garlic bulbs till soft and adding an equal quantity of vinegar to the water in which they have been boiled, and then sugared and boiled down to a syrup. The syrup is then poured over the boiled garlic bulbs, which have been allowed to dry meanwhile, and kept in a jar. Each morning a bulb or two should be taken, with a spoonful of the syrup.

Ear Infections

Wrap a small piece of garlic in some tissue, and insert it into the ear. Leave it there overnight if possible. Pain is almost immediately removed and the infection tends to start clearing up overnight.

Scratchy Throat

Put a small slice of garlic in your mouth and suck on it for 10-15 minutes. You can put it between yjour teeth and cheek, then scratch it with your teeth a little to help stimulate juice from the garlic slice. This juice slides down your throat and removes the pain.

Insect Bites

Garlic can heal the pain caused by insect bites like those of scorpions and centipedes. The juice of fresh garlic mixed with salt can be applied to bruises, sprains and ringworms.

Colds

At the first sign of a cold, chop up 4 cloves of raw garlic and eat or use it as a garnish in soups etc.

Toothache

Cut raw garlic and rub the cut edge on the tooth and gums a couple of times a day to stop toothache.

Warts

Take fresh garlic cloves and crush them; apply to warts until they disappear.

Garlic Breath Tip

Crush a clove or two onto a dessert spoon then add olive oil and down the hatch. You get the benefits of raw garlic with none of the breath issues.

Sinuses

Melt some butter and add minced garlic cloves, spread on toast and eat.

Herpes

Take a garlic clove and cut in half. Eat one half and take the other half and rub into the affected areas. (may sting a little).

Rashes

Use raw garlic juice on rashes and bug bites, it stops the itching immediately.

Coughts

8 to 10 of garlic juice mixed with 2 TBLS of honey four times a day cures a persistent cough.

Tonsillitis

Peel a clove of garlic and cut them in half lengthwise. Boil for a couple of minutes in about 1.5 cup water and add a pinch of salt, teaspoon of butter, a pinch of pepper and sprinkle with nutmeg.

Bloating - Constipation

Cut garlic clove into small pieces. Swallow them all in one go with a little water to cure bloating, stomach cramps and constipation.

Asthma Cure

10 drops of garlic juice with 2 teaspoon of honey cures asthma.

Growing Garlic

Garlic is typically planted in the fall or early winter, though it may also be planted in the early spring in warmer climates.

We advise fall planting for most gardeners. Garlic roots develop during the fall and winter before the ground freezes and by early spring, they start producing foliage.

In areas that get a hard frost, plant garlic about 2 weeks after your first fall frost date, but before the ground freezes. The timing may vary with local climate; the aim is to allow a long enough period before the ground freezes for the plant to develop good roots, but not enough time to for it to form top growth before freezing temperatures set in.

In cooler climates, planting is usually between September and November.

In warm areas with mild winters, you have the option to plant garlic in the fall or in late winter/early spring usually February or March.

Choosing And Preparing A Planting Site

Select a sunny spot.

Garlic likes fertile, well-drained soil with a pH of 6.5 to 7. If your soil is on the thin, sandy side, add healthy additions of compost, plus aged manure or 5-10-10 fertilizer. (Don't use fresh, unprocessed animal manure, as it can transfer diseases.)

For an easy and large harvest, garlic grower Robin Jarry of Hope, Maine, suggests using heavily mulched raised beds, especially in heavy soil. "I plant in raised beds for good drainage, and then mulch with about six inches of old hay after the ground freezes. I never water my garlic I like low-maintenance vegetables!" Raised beds should be two to three feet wide and at least 10 to 12 inches tall.

Lime the soil if you haven't done so recently. Before planting cloves, work couple tablespoons of 5-10-10 complete fertilizer, bone meal or fish meal into the soil several inches below where the base of the garlic will rest.

How To Plant Garlic

Get cloves from a mail order seed company or a local nursery.

Do not use cloves from the grocery store for planting. They may be unsuitable varieties for your area, and most are treated to make their shelf life longer, making them harder to grow.

Select large, healthy cloves, free of disease. The larger the clove, the bigger and healthier the bulb you will get the following summer.

Break apart cloves from the bulb a few days before planting, but keep the papery husk on each individual clove.

Place cloves 2 to 4 inches apart and 2 inches deep, in their upright position (the wide root side facing down and pointed end facing up).

Plant in rows spaced 10 to 14 inches apart.

How To Grow Garlic

Northern gardener's should mulch heavily with straw to ensure proper overwintering. Mulch should be removed in the spring after the threat of frost has passed. (Young shoots can't survive in temps below 20°F / -6°C on their own. Keep them under cover.)

In the spring, as warmer temperatures come, shoots will emerge through the ground.

Cut off any flower shoots that emerge in spring. These may decrease bulb size.

Fertilize garlic in the early spring by side dressing with a nitrogen-heavy fertilizer such as blood meal, chicken manure, or a store-bought pelleted fertilizer.

Fertilize again just before the bulbs begin to swell in response to lengthening daylight (usually early May in most regions).

Weeds should not be a problem until spring. However, keep the planting site well weeded. Garlic doesn't do well with competition it needs all available nutrients!

Garlic is a heavy feeder which requires adequate levels of nitrogen. Fertilize more if you see yellowing leaves.

Water every 3 to 5 days during bulbing (mid-May through June). If May and June are very dry, irrigate to a depth of two feet every eight to 10 days. As mid-June approaches, taper off watering.

Pests/Diseases

Garlic has very few problems with pests in the garden (in fact, its a natural pest repellent), and also very few problems with the diseases that plague other veggies. White rot is one concern, butyou should also keep an eye out for the same pests that plague onions.

White Rot is a fungus that may attack garlic in cool weather. Not much can be done to control or prevent that problem except rotating your crops and cleaning up the area after harvesting. The spores can live in the soil for many years. The fungus affects the base of the leaves and roots.

Harvest/Storage

HOW TO HARVEST GARLIC

Harvest from fall plantings will range from late June to August. In Southern climates, it will depend on your planting date. The clue is to look for yellowing foliage. Harvest when the tops just begin to yellow and fall over, but before they are completely dry.

Before digging up your whole crop, it's time for a sample! Lift a bulb to see if the crop is ready. We often dig up a bulb before the tops are completely yellow (in late June or early July) as some garlic types will be ready earlier. The garlic head will be divided into plump cloves and the skin covering the outside of the bulbs will be thick, dry and papery.

If pulled too early, the bulb wrapping will be thin and disintegrate.

If left in the ground too long, the bulbs sometimes split apart. The skin may also split, which exposes the bulbs to disease and will affect their longevity in storage.

To harvest, carefully dig (don't pull!) up the bulbs with a spade or garden fork. Lift the plants, carefully brush off the soil, and let them cure in an airy, shady, dry spot for two weeks. We hang them upside down on a string in bunches of 4 to 6. Make sure all sides get good air circulation. Be careful not to bruise the garlic or it won't store well.

How To Store Garlic

The bulbs are cured and ready to store when the wrappers are dry and papery and the roots are dry. The root crown should be hard, and the cloves can be cracked apart easily.

Once the garlic bulbs are dry, you can store them. Remove any dirt and trim off any roots or leaves. Keep the wrappers on but remove the dirtiest wrappers. Remove the tops and roots.

Bulbs should be stored in a cool (40°F / 4°C), dark, dry place, and can be kept in the same way for several months. Don't store in your basement if it's moist! Do not store garlic in the refrigerator, either.

The flavor will increase as the bulbs are dried. Properly stored, garlic should last until the next crop is harvested the following summer.

If you plan on planting garlic again next season, save some of your largest, best-formed bulbs to plant again in the fall.

Spacing For Garlic

Recommended varieties

What type of garlic should you plant? There are three types of garlic: Softneck, Hardneck, and Great-headed (Elephant). Most types are about 90 days to harvests, once growth starts.

Hardneck varieties grow one ring of cloves around a stem, there is not a layer of cloves as there is in softneck varieties. They are extremely cold hardy, but do not store as well or long as other varieties. Flavor is milder than softnecks. Common hardneck types include 'Korean Red', 'Duganski', 'Siberian', 'Music', 'Chesnok Red', 'German Red' and 'Spanish Roja'. These varieties produce tiny bulblets at the end of a tall flowering stalk in addition to a fat underground bulb of cloves.

Softneck varieties, like their name suggests, have necks that stay soft after harvest, and therefore are the types that you see braided. Especially recommended for those in warmer climes, as it is\ less winter-hardy than other types. Strong, intense flavor. They tend to grow bigger bulbs because energy is not being diverted to top-set bulblets like hardnecks. Softneck varieties include 'Silverskin', 'Inchelium Red', 'California Early' and 'California Late'.

Great-headed (Elephant) garlic is not recommended if you're looking for a garlic taste. It's less hardy, and more closely related to leeks than other varieties. The flavor is more like onion than traditional garlic. Bulbs and cloves are large, with about 4 cloves to a bulb.

Garlic Recipes

Garlic – whether pickled or pureed, baked or boiled – is the cornerstone of cuisines the world over, featuring in everything from Spanish soups to quince aioli

Baked garlic and shallots with fino

This is perfect for the spring, when the new season's garlic arrives. Its soft cloves – encased in sweet papery casings are gentle in flavour, and the heads can be roasted and eaten whole. Theygo beautifully with roasted shallots. Serve on grilled bread, with a spoonful or two of goat's curd, or as an accompaniment to a simple roast chicken.

Serves 4

- 4 garlic bulbs
- 8 banana shallots
- 5 lemon thyme sprigs (or ordinary thyme)
- 4 bay leaves
- 600ml fresh chicken stock
- 180ml fino sherry

- 50g unsalted butter, in pieces
- 50g parmesan, freshly grated

Salt and black pepper

1. Preheat the oven to 180C/350F/gas mark 4. Slice the garlic bulbs in half horizontally and place in a roasting tray. Halve the shallots, slip off their outer skins and add to the garlic. Season with salt and pepper, then scatter over the lemon thyme and bay leaves.
2. Bring the chicken stock to the boil in a small pan, then pour over the garlic and shallots. Drizzle over the sherry.
3. Cover the tray tightly with foil and roast in the oven for 40 minutes. Remove the foil and return to the oven for a further 15 minutes, until the shallots and garlic are golden brown and the stock has reduced down and thickened. Add the butter and parmesan and stir to combine. Taste, adjust the seasoning, and then serve.

Mellow garlic puree

The longer you cook garlic, the mellower the flavour. If you want more of a punchy puree, only cook for 7 minutes. You can serve this puree with seared pigeon breasts, lamb's kidneys or a sliver of salted anchovies on toast, or with lamb instead of mint sauce.

Serves 4

- 3 garlic bulbs, peeled
- About 200ml milk
- 1 tbsp extra virgin olive oil
- A few drops of sherry vinegar (optional)

Salt and black pepper

1. Place the peeled garlic in a small saucepan, and cover with the milk. Simmer the garlic for 10 minutes, until it is just soft. Add olive oil and salt and pepper.
2. Strain and reserve the milk. Now, with a handheld blender, puree the garlic with the 6tbsp of milk. When smooth, add the sherry vinegar (if using) and check the seasoning.

Quince aioli

This fruity variation of aioli goes especially well with pork and lamb. It's best to use a food processor or mixing bowl when you're dealing with something as dense as membrillo, but if you're just using a pestle and mortar, melt the membrillo down first with a tiny bit of water over a low heat. This will make it easier to incorporate the oil.

Serves 4

- 1 garlic clove
- 250g membrillo (quince paste)
- 150ml oil (equal parts extra virgin olive oil and sunflower oil)

Salt and black pepper

1. Crush the garlic with a little salt in the pestle and mortar.
2. Transfer to a food processor or bowl, and add the membrillo. Blend, and slowly add the oil in a thin stream, resting occasionally, until all the oil is incorporated. Add more salt, pepper and lemon juice to taste.

Caramelised garlic tart with an almond flour base

Sweet caramelised garlic and butternut squash combine with creamy goat's cheese and the aniseed flavours of tarragon to make a delicious, uniquely flavoured tart with a twist – we use ground almonds to make a nutritious and gluten-free crust.

Serves 4-5

For the pastry

- 375g ground almonds
- 1 tsp sea salt
- ½ tsp bicarbonate of soda
- ½ tbsp maple syrup
- 30g butter, softened
- 2 eggs

For the filling

- 250g butternut squash, skin on, deseeded
- 3 medium bulbs garlic, cloves peeled
- 30g butter
- 1 tbsp maple syrup
- 1 tbsp cider vinegar
- 2 eggs
- 7 tbsp full-fat yoghurt
- 60g mature cheddar, grated
- 70g goat's cheese
- 3 tsp chopped tarragon

Salt and black pepper

1. Preheat the oven to 180C/350F/gas mark 4 and roast the butternut squash in the oven for 40-50 minutes, cut-side up, until cooked through and tender.

2. Mix the pastry ingredients together and roll into a 3mm-thick disc between two pieces of parchment paper. Line a 24cm ceramic tart dish with the almond pastry, trimming away the excess. Line with greaseproof paper, fill with baking beans and put into the fridge for 20 minutes.

3. Bake for 10 minutes, remove the beans and bake for 10 minutes more. Set aside.

4. Meanwhile put the garlic in a small pan with a few tbsp of water. Simmer for a few minutes until almost tender. Add the butter, increase the heat and cook until the water has evaporated and the garlic is starting to brown.

5. Add the maple syrup, cider vinegar and a pinch of sea salt and simmer for 10 minutes, until most of the liquid has evaporated and the cloves are coated in dark syrup.

6. Peel the skin from the squash, chop into 2cm pieces and arrange in the tart base. Whisk the eggs, yoghurt and grated cheddar together with a pinch of salt and a few good grinds of black pepper and pour over the squash.

7. Scatter pieces of goat's cheese and caramelised garlic over the tart, drizzle over the syrup and sprinkle with the tarragon.

8. Reduce heat to 170C/325F/gas mark 3 and bake the tart for 30 minutes, until it sets and the top goes golden brown. Eat warm or at room temperature with a crisp seasonal salad.

Tofu steak

Cooked with a combination of garlic and leeks and dressed with banno soy sauce, this dish has the most amazing aroma.

Serves 4

For the banno soy sauce

- 100ml mirin
- 300ml soy sauce
- 10cm-piece konbu seaweed, wiped of any salty deposits

For the tofu steaks

- 600g soft/silken tofu
- 8 garlic cloves, finely chopped
- 4-5 tbsp plain flour
- 3-4 tbsp sunflower or vegetable oil

Salt and black pepper

To serve

- 25g fresh ginger, finely grated
- 50g spring onion, finely sliced
- A small handful of katsuobushi (dried fish flakes optional)

1. To make the banno soy sauce, bring the mirin to the boil in a small saucepan, and then reduce the heat to low and cook for a further 2-3 minutes to burn off the alcohol. Remove from the heat and add the soy sauce and konbu. Leave to cool, then refrigerate.
2. Drain the tofu and cut into four pieces, wiping off any water with a paper towel.
3. Season the tofu on both sides with salt and pepper, then cover with the garlic.
4. Lightly coat the tofu pieces in flour.
5. Heat the oil in a frying pan and, when hot, add the tofu, cooking until it is crispy and browned on both sides.
6. Garnish with ginger and spring onions and top with a sprinkling of katsuobushi, if using. Dress with the banno soy sauce to taste. Any soy sauce that's left over will

keep in the fridge in an airtight container for up to 3 weeks.

Roasted Garlic And Butternut Squash Hummus With Goat's Cheese

The base of this hummus is made of butternut squash, which creates a sweet, light dip that is complemented by two sweet and aromatic roasted garlic bulbs.

Serves 4-6

- A small/medium butternut squash (700-900g)
- 4 tbsp olive oil, plus extra to rub on the squash and garlic and to serve
- 2 garlic bulbs – about 25-30 cloves
- Lemon zest from ½ lemon and a generous squeeze of juice
- 2 tbsp tahini
- 10 sprigs of fresh thyme, leaves torn from stems
- A handful of flat-leaf parsley, finely chopped
- 50g creamy goat's cheese

Salt and black pepper

1. Preheat oven to 200C/400F/gas mark 6. Cut the butternut squash in half and remove the seeds. Rub it with olive oil and a pinch of salt and pepper. Bake in the oven for 45-60 minutes, depending on size.
2. Split the garlic into individual cloves but keep the peel on. Rub them with a little olive oil and bake for around 20-25 minute's beside the squash. Keep an eye on the garlic cloves they should be tender and golden, not hard and burned.
3. When everything is done, scoop out the flesh of the butternut squash and peel the garlic cloves. Place both in a blender and add the lemon zest and juice and tahini. Pulse until the garlic and squash are well combined. Transfer to a bowl.
4. Add half the chopped parsley and season to taste with salt and pepper.
5. Serve with crumbled goat's cheese, a splash of olive oil and the rest of the fresh herbs scattered on top.

Indonesian Garlic Fried Chicken

Of the many versions of ayam goreng (fried chicken) in Indonesia, this is the most delicious crispy and toffee-brown on the outside, sweet and succulent on the inside thanks to its unusualpre-frying marinade of garlic and palm vinegar.

Serves 4

1. whole chicken (1.4-1.6kg) cut into 10 pieces or 1.4kg chicken wings, thighs and/or drumsticks
- 8 garlic cloves, peeled and smashed
- 250ml palm cider or rice vinegar
- 1½ tsp sea salt

Peanut oil, for frying

2. Rinse the chicken under cold water, drain well and pat dry with a paper towel. Set aside In a large bowl, combine the garlic, vinegar and salt. Add the chicken and combine well. Cover in clingfilm and leave to marinate in the fridge for 1-2 hours, stirring once or twice to ensure the marinade coats every piece.
3. Remove the chicken pieces from the marinade and pat them thoroughly dry with a paper towel, gently squeezing each piece to remove excess liquid. Set aside.
4. Add oil to a depth of 2½cm in a 30cm frying pan and place over a medium-high heat until hot but not smoking. Gently slide as many of the chicken pieces into

the oil as will fit without touching (you'll probably need to fry the chicken in two batches). After about 10 minutes, when the chicken has turned deep golden brown and crispy, turn it over and continue to fry – it should take 20-25 minutes in total. Test by poking a fork into the thickest portion and pressing down on it   the juices should run clear, not pink.

5. Remove the chicken pieces and let them drain on a wire rack or paper towels for a few minutes before transferring to a serving platter. Serve immediately.

Korean pickled garlic

Maneul jangajji is a traditional side dish in Korea. The garlic cloves are first soaked in a vinegar brine for a few days, before being pickled in a soy brine. Through this two-step process, the garlic loses much of its pungent bite and becomes slightly sweet and tangy.

Makes 1 large jar

- 500g fresh garlic (about 8–9 whole heads)

For the vinegar brine

- 150ml vinegar
- 1 tbsp sea salt

- 400ml water

For the soy brine

- 150ml soy sauce
- 60ml vinegar
- 3 tbsp sugar
- 400ml water

1. Separate the garlic cloves. Soak in hot water for 30 minutes or longer, which will help the skins come off easily. Peel and remove the root ends with a small knife. Rinse and drain. Add to a large sterilised pickling jar.
2. Stir the vinegar brine ingredients together until the salt has dissolved and pour enough over the garlic cloves to submerge them. Secure the lid and leave to stand at room temperature for 5-7days.
3. Bring the soy brine ingredients to a boil, and gently boil for 5 minutes over a medium heat. Allow to cool completely.
4. Drain the vinegar brine from the jar. Pour the cooled soy brine over the garlic cloves. Make sure all the garlic cloves are submerged. Close the lid tightly and leave to stand at room temperature for 2 weeks. The garlic can

be eaten at this point, but it will taste better as it matures. Refrigerate after opening. The garlic cloves will keep for a few months.

Sopa De Ajo

This is a noble and sustaining soup found throughout Spain, especially in Castilla-La Mancha. Despite regional variations, the main ingredients of this soup are always the same: garlic, eggs, bread and paprika.

Serves 4

- 4 tbsp olive oil
- 4-5 large garlic bulbs, broken into cloves with skin kept on
- 100g cooking chorizo, cut into little pieces
- 1 tsp fresh thyme leaves
- ½ tsp sweet smoked Spanish paprika
- 1 litre chicken stock
- 4 eggs
- 8 slices ciabatta or sourdough bread, toasted and torn into rough pieces

Salt and black pepper

1. Heat the oil in a saucepan over a low heat. Add the garlic and fry gently for 15-20 minutes, stirring often, until the skins are golden brown and the flesh is soft. Remove with a slotted spoon.

2. When slightly cool, squeeze out the sweet garlic flesh by hand (discarding the skins), puree and set aside.

3. Meanwhile, add the chorizo to the pan and fry until crisp and caramelised.

4. Add the thyme, fry for a few seconds, then add the pureed garlic. Stir well, add the paprika and pour on the chicken stock. Bring to a gentle simmer and season to taste.

5. About 2 minutes before serving, poach the eggs in the soup and add the toasted bread. Taste once more and serve immediately.

Green Garlic And Scapes Risotto

If you live in a green-garlic and scape-less society you can use a bulb of normal garlic and a leek instead of the scapes (stems).

Serves 2

- 40g butter
- 1 tbsp olive oil
- 1 shallot, finely chopped

- 4 rashers pancetta, thinly sliced
- 1 bulb of new, young garlic, cloves peeled and halved lengthways
- 100g arborio rice
- 500ml chicken stock
- Half a head of romaine lettuce, chopped
- 1 bunch garlic scapes (or 1 leek), finely chopped
- Juice of ½ a lime
- 75g frozen green peas
- 4 tbsp parmesan, grated

1. In a saucepan melt two-thirds of the butter with the olive oil. Add the shallot, pancetta and green garlic cloves. Cook for about 5 minutes without allowing them to colour.
2. Add the rice and stir thoroughly for a minute or so. Now add the warm stock, a ladleful at a time, stirring in between and allowing a few minutes for the rice to cook before adding the next ladleful. After about 10 minutes add the chopped lettuce and stir.
3. Once the lettuce has wilted, add the chopped scapes or leek.

4. Add the lime juice and stir in the peas. Check the rice and add a little more water if needed. Cook for a few minutes more, stirring continuously, until the peas are hot and the rice is tender.

Conclusion

The beneficial effect of garlic preparations on lipids and blood pressure extends also to platelet function, thus providing a wider potential protection of the cardiovascular system through its major effects on cholestrol reduction.

Made in the USA
Las Vegas, NV
06 December 2023

82219297R00036